INVISIBLE

INVISIBLE

J.R. Solonche

Five Oaks Press
FIVE-OAKS-PRESS.COM

Copyright ©2017 J.R. Solonche
All rights reserved. First print edition.

Five Oaks Press
Newburgh, NY 12550
five-oaks-press.com
editor@five-oaks-press.com

ISBN: 978-1-944355-29-6

Cover and Book Design: Lynn Houston

Printed in the United States of America

ACKNOWLEDGMENTS

The American Scholar: "A Photograph of Charlie Chaplin and Albert Einstein" and "Schopenhauer at the Englischer Hof: A Monologue"

Atlanta Review: "Shaker Chair"

Blue Unicorn: "Isaac"

Carbon Culture Review: "The Poem of the Future"

Cutthroat: "Invisible"

Dark Matter Journal: "The Anti-Tyger"

Free Verse: "A Hawk with a Broken Wing is a Hawk Broken"

JAMA: "Angina"

Lily: "Gathering for Alice"

Monongahela Review: "Eight Short Speeches for Cain"

Mudfish: "The Horses"

The New Criterion: "Over There"

Offcourse Literary Journal: "Coyote," "In the House of Salt, Every Window is an Open Wound," and "Twenty-one Attempts at the William Matthews Challenge to Ruin, with the Least Possible Change, a Famous Line of Poetry"

Poet Lore: "Acrobat," "E.D. at the Academy," and "Rhinoceros Head"

Poetry Northwest: "The Sugar Loaf Mastodon"

Poetry Quarterly: "The History of Gold"

Rattle: "The Lover of Stone"

Red River Review: "Brando"

Review Americana: "A Young Poet and an Old Poet"

Visiting Frost: Poems Inspired by the Life and Work of Robert Frost: "Worse"

Wordsmith: "Two Portraits by Mathew Brady"

Yankee Magazine: "Einstein's Last Words"

CONTENTS

A Hawk with a Broken Wing is a Hawk Broken 5

Al Pacino 6

A Photograph of Muhammad Ali and Marianne Moore 7

Acrobat 8

Adam's Dream 9

Brando 10

Bruce Springsteen's Guitar 11

Coltrane on Soprano 12

Columbus 13

Coyote 14

E. D. at the Academy 15

Eight Short Speeches for Cain 16

Einstein's Last Words 18

The Story of the Prophet Elisha, the Little Children,
and the Two She-Bears 19

False Messiah 20

Found Poem with Variations 21

Gathering for Alice 22

The History of Gold 23

Hamlet's Blues 25

In the House of Salt, Every Window is an Open Wound 26

Invisible 29

Isaac 30

Lear 31

A Photograph of William Carlos Williams 32

Prospero 33

Rhinoceros Head 34

Shaker Chair 35

Spinosa 36

The Sugar Loaf Mastodon 38

The Anti-Tyger 40

The Greatest Names in Poetry 41

The Horses 44

The Lover of Stone 46

The Poem of the Future 47

Two Portraits by Mathew Brady 48

When the Buddha was 80 Years Old 50

Worse 51

A Young Poet and an Old Poet 52

Twenty-two Attempts at the William Matthews Challenge to Ruin, with the Least Possible Change, a Famous Line of Poetry 53

If Edgar Allan Poe Had Written "Trees" 56

If Wallace Stevens Had Written "Trees" 57

If Robert Frost Had Written "Trees" 59

If Emily Dickinson Had Written "Trees" 60

If Walt Whitman Had Written "Trees" 61

If William Blake Had Written "Trees" 62

If T.S. Eliot Had Written "Trees" 63

A Photograph of Charlie Chaplin and Albert Einstein 64

Over There 65

Angina 66

Percy Shelley to a Skylark 67

Schopenhauer at the Englischer Hof: A Monologue 68

One of the Trapped Chilean Miners Was a Poet 70

Zeppo 72

A HAWK WITH A BROKEN WING IS A HAWK BROKEN

A hawk with a broken wing is a hawk broken.
A broken bird.

It gives up the sky for a perch perpetual.
It forgets feathers but remembers what talons are for.

A branch chewed half through by claws is its prey.
A broken hawk hops from low to lower.

A broken hawk jumps from lower to low.
A broken hawk has a broken eye also.

It has a short sky that does not require a hawk's unbroken eye.
A canopy with no view of the sky is their kindest kindness.

AL PACINO

The pair of glasses he is wearing is not a pair of glasses.
It is a pair of tennis shoes playing a pair of glasses.

Those gold chains around his neck are not gold chains.
They are over-the-hill porn stars portraying gold chains.

That is not a shirt, buttons open. That is not a bare chest.
The shirt is an umbrella, heavily made-up. The bare chest is a knee,

heavily made-up. The buttons are a zipper, heavily made-up.
That is not Al Pacino's mouth forming the letter *W*.

That is a hand playing the role of his mouth. And that
is not the letter *W*. That is a stunt letter *M* standing on its head.

A PHOTOGRAPH OF MUHAMMED ALI
AND MARIANNE MOORE

He is rubbing his chin
with his left hand, as though
rubbing a magic lamp.

Next to him, at
the restaurant table,
a little uncomfortable,

a little unhappy,
gazing off into
the nowhere between

one world and another,
she is the genie who has
just bubbled up out of his ear.

ACROBAT

So supple, so pliable,
she seems to have no skeleton,
or one made of rubber.

Human origami,
folded into a stork,
balancing on one leg.

Unfolded, refolded
into a sequined
quadruped, head

in the center
of a square of feet.
Arched over, arched

under, bent and re-bent,
stretched to the breaking point but
never breaking.

This is
how the rest of us
contort our souls.

ADAM'S DREAM

First there was this strange sensation.
It felt like a finger running along my ribs.
It was quick, firm, with neither pleasure nor pain.
Then I was lying on my back.
A great tree took root between my legs.
In a moment it grew to its full height,
swaying in the wind.
Then it exploded into a glorious crown of fruit.
An angel of the Lord came with a flaming sword.
The angel of the Lord burned the tree to ashes.
I scooped the ashes up into the cup of my hands.
I rubbed the ashes into the skin of my chest and shoulders.
I rubbed the ashes into the skin of my arms and legs.
I found myself in a new place.
There was not a tree nor a bush nor any green thing.
The earth was red and hard beneath my feet.
But I was not alone in that new place.
Behind me I heard laughter and weeping.
I heard laughter and weeping behind me.

BRANDO

He's a box.
He is wrapped in a tee shirt.
The tee shirt is a little too tight.
He wants you to see the shape of the box.

The arms of the box are akimbo.
The right hand of the box is under the left bicep.
The right hand is pushing the left bicep toward you.
That way it looks bigger, more impressive, sexier.

The left eye of the box says, *Open me.*
The right eye of the box says, *If you dare.*
Both eyes of the box say, *Look but do not touch.*
The box has a nose, but it is made of putty.

The box has a mouth, but it is painted on.
The box has a forehead.
The forehead looks like a third bicep.
Or does the box want his biceps to resemble two foreheads?

The box is bulging his forehead at you.
He does this by looking out from under his boxy brows.
He wants you to know there is a brain in there.
He wants you to know it is a big brain, a sexy brain.

He wants you to know his brain is bigger than yours.
He wants you to know his brain is sexier than yours.
So he points it at you, his forehead.
It is the same as telling you his biceps are bigger than yours.

This box wants you to understand something.
He wants you to understand he can beat you any way he wants.
He can beat you with his biceps.
He can beat you with his brains.

Other than that, it is hard to tell what this box wants.
It is a mystery box.
It is a heavy box.
It is an empty box.

BRUCE SPRINGSTEEN'S GUITAR

is white
is pure white
is pure dominant, pure tonic

is white
is snow, is ice
is a glacier glissando

is white
is a swan
is a swan with a straight-as-an-arrow neck

is white
is lily white
is a lily pressed and dried in a book

is white
is white whale white
is Ahab caught in the web of strings

is white
is white hot
is dead white, dead-center white

is white
is bridal gown white
is the bride of rock and roll

is white
is ghost white
is the ghost of a blue guitar

COLTRANE ON SOPRANO

His
eyes are
so closed
they're op
en. From the
top of his he
ad, he sees the
music coming
at him eleven
notes at a time.
He must squee
ze them all thro
ugh this narrow
tongue flick of a
horn, this squeal
er, whiner, sopra
no, diva of a high
pitched saxophone.
Flurries of fingere
d-key-fingers indis
tinguishable from eac
h other, strike the honey
from the stone. O, blurry pain
and slurry sorrow suck the merci
ful marrow from this brass-gold bone.

COLUMBUS

Columbus changed his mind.
The world is not round,

after all, he said in his diary,
It is not a ball,

not a globe.
No, the world is shaped

like a pear, he said in his diary.
It is a woman's breast,

and this mountain
on this east coast of India

is the highest point,
the nipple atop

the breast of the world,
and these waters

spilling down from it,
its milk, he said in his diary,

licking his lips.

COYOTE

When I dashed out across the road in front of your car, I timed it perfectly.

I knew what I was doing.

I am a coyote, after all.

But I wanted you to think I was a dog.

I can make myself look like one when I want to.

I wanted you to exclaim, *Hey, stupid dog. You almost got killed!*

Then I wanted you to think I was a red fox.

I can make myself look like one when I want to.

I wanted you to exclaim, *Hey, fox. You almost bought it, you idiot!*

Then when I all but disappeared into the trees,

showing you only my tail,

I wanted you to know who I really was.

I can make myself look like who I really am when I want to.

I wanted you to exclaim, *Holy shit. What's a fucking coyote doing around here?*

And you did.

After all, gringo, I am a coyote.

E. D. AT THE ACADEMY

In school I was rebellious.
I was a No Hoper.
The Headmistress

gave me a job, to wipe
the knives in the dining hall.
Only the knives.

Nothing else.
But I wiped a spoon
or two behind her back.

And a fork once.
I left after a year.
I had learned everything

they had to teach.
As for grammar. Well,
dash it all!

EIGHT SHORT SPEECHES FOR CAIN

1. To Abel

I was the first to be born in pain. Not them. Not you. What did they know? Our father was asleep. Our mother was unconscious. I am the first to live without having known the garden. Not you. They never speak of it. Except sometimes at night, before sleep, while he is adding wood to the fire, I hear them whispering. You are asleep. You do not hear them whispering. If you ever tell them I said this, you prick, I'll kill you.

2. To God

I have thought about this brother and I do not understand. Why did we need another? Did we not bring forth with our hands the fruits of the earth? Did we not bring forth with our toil the bread of the earth? Did we not in all things obey your word? Then it must be you were not pleased with us as we were. Then it must be your word she obeyed and not his. Your word and not hers. Your word and not mine.

3. To Eve

When I asked you, you said it was because I was lonely. But I was not lonely. I skipped with the lambs in the fields. The goats were my companions. When I asked you again, you said it was because we needed another in the fields. We needed another to turn the hard stones from the earth. I said it was not so. I said we do these things ourselves. I said we needed no other. I was not lonely. I was not lonely. Then you turned and went away from me. I was afraid. I trembled.

4. To Adam

This is your doing. You are to blame. You should have disobeyed. What would be the punishment this time? He has used all the punishments. There are none left. She is weak. But you are weaker, weaker than a woman.

5. To Abel

I did not think he would look for me so soon. I thought he would find you first and breathe the breath back into your body. Did he not breathe the breath of life into our father? He could have done the same for you before seeking me out to ask where you were. He knew where you were. He can do it now. Now. Doesn't he know you are my offering? He can do it now. Now. Now.

6. To Seth

I know you. I am Cain. Your brother. The brother you have never met. Who slew Abel. The brother you never knew. I know they told you. You should be grateful. You should thank me for what I did. Had I not done it, you would not have been born. You would not now be standing before me, gazing on this mark upon my forehead. You should be grateful. Seth, you have her eyes. As I do. Kiss my right hand, you little shit. It held the stone that gave you life.

7. To His Wife, Mother of Enoch

If it offends you, I will wrap a linen cloth around it.

8. To Enoch

My son, do not be afraid. This mark is also his mark. The marker also must bear the punishment. His hand must also burn. My son, when you were born, I took you from your mother. I lifted you up to my eyes, and I wept with joy. On your forehead was nothing. Not a mark. Not a spot. Your brow was white and clean as the wool of the lamb. Enoch, my son, I will build a city and name it for you. Then I will die in peace.

EINSTEIN'S LAST WORDS

>Einstein died on April 18, 1955, attended
>by a nurse who could not understand
>his last words, which he spoke in German.

Surely it must have been a simple thing,
that sort of phrase the ordinary old
would say, child-like, such as "More light" or "Bring
me, please, water" or "Close the door" or "Hold

my hand" or "I was wrong" or "What's the time?"
Perhaps it was a line or two of verse
from *Faust,* or a nonsense nursery rhyme
that curved around to close his universe.

And if all it was was a little joke,
of a man meeting God in Paradise,
and God laughed at it, even then he spoke
to himself. Two silences must suffice.

THE STORY OF THE PROPHET ELISHA, THE LITTLE CHILDREN AND THE TWO SHE-BEARS

In the Bible, there is a story about little children who are torn apart by bears.

The story goes like this. Elisha, a prophet of the Lord, was bald on the top of his head. Although he had a long and flowing beard, he had not a single hair upon his head. One day, on the way to Bethel where he was going, Elisha was jeered at by little children who ran after him crying, "Go up, you baldhead! Go up, you baldhead!" Now, Elisha was very proud of his long, flowing beard, but he was also very sensitive about his bald head. Also, it so happens that Elisha did not like children. So Elisha turned around to face the little children, and Elisha cursed them in the name of the Lord with a terrible curse. Immediately, two she-bears came out of the woods and tore apart forty-two of the children who had been running after Elisha on his way.

That is how the story goes. But there is more to the story than the Bible tells, and this is how it goes. There were actually forty-three children who ran after Elisha on his way to Bethel where he was going that day. Forty-two of the children were indeed torn apart by the two she-bears that came out of the woods, but the forty-third child, who was a boy, the littlest child, was not torn apart. He hid himself behind a tree, and he escaped the claws of the two she-bears. And he saw everything that happened to the forty-two children and remembered all that he saw and all he heard. The name of this boy, the name of this forty-third child, was Yeshua. He wandered in the woods and in the desert for forty-two years of his life, eating what nut and berries and honey he could gather, and he grew his hair long, and he never cut even a single hair on his head, but never allowed a beard to grow, plucking each hair as it appeared on his chin. Yeshua hated all the prophets of the Lord, and when he was forty-three years of age, he founded a religion only for children.

FALSE MESSIAH

We have stopped
the full-page ads
in the newspaper
and taken his picture

down from the signs
in Brooklyn.
We have cancelled
the charters to the Holy Land.

We have shorn our side-locks
and rent our cassocks.
We have sanctified our kitchens
and shut in our women.

We have ordered new ink,
new paper, new books.
We have told the carpenters
to measure oak for new chairs.

We have screwed new bulbs tight
into the sockets of our lights.
We have begged our children
for their forgiveness. Amen.

FOUND POEM WITH VARIATIONS

Paganini is supposed to have said
that Stradivari "only used the wood
on trees on which nightingales sang."

Frost is supposed to have said
that Dickinson "only used the paper
from trees on which butterflies were born."

Pound is supposed to have said
that Whitman "only used the paper
from trees under whose boughs couples copulated."

Moore is supposed to have said
that Frost "only used the paper
from New Hampshire maple trees."

Tennyson is supposed to have said
that Blake "only used the paper
from trees in which angels sat."

Creeley is supposed to have said
that Ginsberg "only used the paper
from the same trees Whitman used."

GATHERING FOR ALICE

It is simple.
In the center of the room is a table.
A candle is on the table.
A vase is on the table.

In the vase are yellow daffodils.
In the vase are white daffodils.
It is spring.
They burn yellow like yellow candles.

They burn white like white candles.
Sunlight shines through the windows.
The windows burn white.
The walls of the room are white.

We who are quietly gathered
quietly remember her.
We who are softly gathered
softly remember her.

She was simple.
For ninety-five years she was a candle.
For ninety-five years
the storms could not extinguish her.

For ninety-five years she was simple.
Now she is simpler still.
She is simpler than candles.
She is simpler than flowers.

She is simpler than years.
She is simpler than windows,
than sunlight through windows.
She is simple.

THE HISTORY OF GOLD

The first to find it smelled it first.

Like everything else.

Then put it to his mouth to taste.

Like everything else.

Made a face.

Decided it was not good to eat.

Made a different face.

Did not toss it aside on the heap.

Of flint flake.

Of pit ash.

Of thigh bone sucked.

Kept it.

For it was shiny.

Kept it.

For it was yellow.

For it was as yellow as the sun.

For it was a piece of the sun.

Looked up.

Shaded his eyes with his hand.

Saw a hole in the sun.

Smelled it again.

Kept it.

For it was heavy in his hand.

For it was to hold onto.

Kept it.

For it could be useful somehow.

Kept it.

How?

Around the neck?

Around the wrist?

Around a finger?

Kept it.

For what?

Kept it.

As what?

Kept it.

For it was to hold onto.

Forever.

Kept it.

For it was to kill for.

Forever.

HAMLET'S BLUES

My daddy is dead and my momma's remarried.
I say my daddy is dead and my momma she's remarried.
I want t'go back to school.

I got them t'be or not t'be blues.
Oh I got them old t'be or not t'be blues.
I feel like such a fool.

My daddy's ghost done told me.
I say my daddy's white ghost he done told me
My Uncle Claude him done kill to rule.

I got them t'be or not t'be blues.
Oh I got them old t'be or not t'be blues.
I want t'go back to school.

I love a sweet gal named Ophelia.
I say I love a sweet gal by the name of Ophelia.
But she's just her daddy's tool.

I got them t'be or not t'be blues.
Oh I got them old t'be or not t'be blues.
I feel like such a fool.

I got a bosom friend named Horatio.
I say I got a bosom friend and his name's Horatio.
Damn, I think I love him too.

I got them t'be or not t'be blues.
Oh I got them old t'be or not t'be blues.
I got t'go back to school.

IN THE HOUSE OF SALT, EVERY WINDOW IS AN OPEN WOUND

In the house of salt, every window is an open wound.
In the house of fire, there is no light.

In the house of dreams, there is no rest.
In the house of women, there is no opportunity.

In the house of steel, there is no need for iron.
In the house of laughter, there is no need for jokes.

In the house of ice, there is nothing to drink.
In the house of the moon, the sun is the devil.

In the house of nightmares, there is no mercy.
In the house of butterflies, moths are not welcome.

In the house of mirrors, your face is your life's work.
In the house of piety, there is not enough pity to go around.

In the house of toys, there is no need for wisdom.
In the house of bells, there is no need for conversation.

In the house of heroes, the story of the coward gets longer with every telling.
In the house of hell, only the ceiling is fireproof.

In the house of the sky, you must never look down.
In the house of circles, there is no need to think straight.

In the house of the future, you will live like there is no today.
In the house of the valley, your dreams are the echoes of your days.

In the house of numbers, all names end with a question mark.
In the house of rain, you reach your destiny only by river.

In the house of history, you will carry 10,000 flags.
In the house of honey, only silk flowers may be arranged in the vases.

In the house of wolves, who will tell the bedtime stories?
In the house of hours, minutes are your parents, seconds are your grandparents.

In the house of clocks, calendars are holy scripture.
In the house of nails, not forever can you hide your hammer.

In the house of hawks, you must perfect the art of disguise.
In the house of music, there are more secrets than keepers of secrets.

In the house of courage, there is no need for fathers.
In the house of books, there is no need for doors.

In the house of miracles, magic is strangled in the cradle.
In the house of dance, only the crippled may walk.

In the house of roses, where do the daisies sleep?
In the house of hair, the comb hangs over the fireplace and the razor blades are bronzed.

In the house of sunshine, the shadows never lose their edge.
In the house of prayer, the cries of the hungry forever go unheeded.

In the house of comedy, the worst of tragedies is silence.
In the house of hope, the light switches read *on* and *on*.

In the house of lost causes, the soapboxes are in the garage, neatly stacked.
In the house of flattery, how do you know which one to imitate?

In the house of happy endings, the sadder the beginning the better.
In the house of impossibilities, forty times forty is not time enough.

In the house of strong opinions, the facts are the first to leave the room and the last to return.
In the house of mistaken identities, all love is irksome.

In the house of secrets, blackmail is for breakfast.
In the house of hypocrisy, the name on the mailbox is *Politics*.

In the house of paradox, the poet is always welcome.
In the house of poetry, truth lives in the basement, language in the attic.

In the house of certainty, the foundation rests on the skulls of the mistaken.
In the house of dust, death feels right at home.

INVISIBLE

1.

When they are thirteen, all boys want to be invisible.

2.

The physicists tell us ninety percent of the universe is invisible.

3.

Should it not occur to us that since the greatest part of our lives is lived in our minds, we too are ninety percent invisible?

4.

When we watch the willow branches stirred by the wind,
when we watch the cumulus clouds billow in the wind,
when we watch the paper kite strain the string in the wind,
three times we ponder the invisible.

5.

Of all the incredible things about my cat Hector,
the most incredible is how he sees the invisible.

6.

Except when it is reflecting something else, glass,
the most miraculous of materials, so too the most
metaphorical, is naturally visibly invisible.

7.

And then there is godmother death, her gray hair,
her false teeth, her cane, whom we know from birth,
so familiar to us she is all but invisible.

ISAAC

They woke no earlier than usual,
just dawn, as though it were another day
of tending flocks. At once he saw the way
was different, though, not toward the jagged wall

of date palms, and through it past the rock-fall.
Where were they going then? When would he say?
He looked. His father's look did not betray
intent or doubt. It was a stern white wall.

He nearly fainted when he saw the knife.
He fainted when he smelled the ram's fat burn,
the smoke like black wool curling from the stone.

That night he dreamt he was a man with wife
and child. The angel came, stony white, stern,
and his face was flame. He said, *Wake your son.*

LEAR

Even before it begins, you sense what is wrong.
You feel the tug of imbalance,
the ominous pull of the missing.

Yet all looks correct.
Everything is in place.
Here is the resigning king, the still reigning father.

Here are the daughters, Cordelia, Goneril, Regan.
Here is Glouster.
Here are Edgar, Kent, the fool, suitors and soldiers.

So it is done.
So he is done for.
No mother, no wife, no queen is here to command:

Lear, no more of this.
No more of this nonsense.
Hear?

A PHOTOGRAPH OF WILLIAM CARLOS WILLIAMS

He is laughing,
perhaps at what someone is saying,
but more likely at what he is saying.
His face is laughing,
his whole face is laughing,
his mouth, his eyes behind his glasses,
his eyebrows above his glasses duplicating
the curve of his glasses,
his chin, all are laughing.
His necktie is laughing
tucked under his collar which
is laughing around his neck which
is laughing.
His necktie is laughing at both ends.
His shirt is laughing
out from behind his necktie
and the two shirt pockets, one
buttoned and one unbuttoned are laughing,
but the unbuttoned pocket is laughing the louder.
His jacket is laughing,
a big belly laugh all around him.
His hands are laughing,
one hand laughing in his pants' pocket,
the other hand laughing on his waist, holding
his belt which is smiling and in a moment will laugh.

PROSPERO

So every third thought
shall be the grave. But
what shall every first
thought be, and every
second thought? A blow-
job? A glass of wine?
His grandchild on his
knee? A nap in the sun?
Or as Dustin Hoffman
said about retirement,
a good baked potato
and a good crap?

RHINOCEROS HEAD

He looks as though he hasn't slept
in weeks, the brown glass eyes softly sad,
the skin beneath folded and sagged.

He wasn't meant to be seen
from such an unnatural angle,
we down here gazing at him

up there above us on the wall.
We want to reach up and rub his chin.
We want to toss a hat onto his horn.

Sweetness, all sweetness he is,
like a great, wrinkled gray rose,
with a shark's fin for a thorn.

SHAKER CHAIR

Ballerina of a chair.
Chair *en point*.
Chair on tip-toe to be taller.
Anorexic, thin-as-a-rail chair.

Haiku chair.
Pure and simple chair, pure and simple.
Lithe chair.
Light chair, lighter than air.

Shrewd chair.
Stern chair.
Stiff, stiff-necked chair.
No nonsense chair.

Chair straight to the point of its four points.
Chair all business of going about
its father's business
of form following function following faith.

Austere chair.
Such soft-spoken austerity.
Severe chair.
Such soft-spoken severity.

Discreet chair.
The very soul of discretion.
Stick figure chair
for the stick figure father to sit in.

Secret chair.
Open chair.
Open secret of chairs.
Spare chair with nothing to spare.

SPINOSA

When I was twenty-four, my reasoned faith
was seen as threatening the Jewish world
of Amsterdam, my world. In the rabbis' eyes,

I was a heretic, traitor to the God
of Israel, the God of history. My light
was their darkness, and my philosophy

was dangerous, a calumny to faith.
When the rabbis questioned me, I closed my eyes
but answered honestly—*Yes, God*

has a body. God's body is the world.
Yes, angels might be merely tricks of light,
hallucinations. Yes, philosophy

if true to itself, denies a God
who says," You are the Chosen of the world."
They offered to buy my philosophy.

They called it an annuity. In my eyes,
it was a bribe to be silent on faith.
Believe, they said, but not in the daylight.

I refused, of course, and left the dim light
of the synagogue. My orthodox world
was unsatisfied. My intolerant faith

demanded excommunication. My God
became a God who turns away his eyes.
I would not bargain with philosophy,

so again I was called before the faith-
ful when the synagogue blazed with candlelight,
and the shofar wailed. While a thousand eyes

watched, the candles, one by one, were snuffed, the world
unmade, until they cursed with a philosophy
of curses, and only darkness and God

and Chaos remained before my eyes.
So I was accursed in the sight of God
and in the sight of men. But the burden was light.

I lived with a family of the Christian faith.
I taught the daughter some philosophy
and ground lenses to earn my way in the world.

My burden was light. The great of the world
came to talk philosophy and faith,
and I made lenses for men's eyes to see God.

THE SUGAR LOAF MASTODON

Imagine the farmer's sheer surprise as he struck
the skull, or pelvic bone, or tusk
with the point of the plow, and it was not another stone
to curse, to lift out and roll aside.

Which part was the first to see the light
after those millenia?
The yard-wide grin, every tooth in place?
The whimsy of tail?

The romanesque arch of backbone?
The ribs like a whales's baleen?
The tusks, so uselessly huge, the body's bulk
seems nothing more than counterweight?

We know it was alive once, walked the earth we walk,
breathed the air we breathe,
died the death we die,
yet it wears a man-made look,

the look of antique wood, varnished and dark.
And we think it should have once had wheels,
wheels with iron spokes and an iron rim and been
drawn by oxen, too graceless for horses' work.

Or it should have been the scale model
of something many times its size that the pharaohs
never got around to build.
Or it should have been an armature,

a frame over which purple velvet and quilted satin
were draped, embroidered in gold thread,
bespangled, tasseled, and fringed,
between the tusks, a potentate's pillow.

Or it should have been a siege-engine,
a primitive tank armored in stiff leather
and copper plates.
Or a farm machine, an ice age harvester.

We do we scarcely glance
as we pass the glass?
Do we remember a musky smell?
Do we remember a taste?

THE ANTI-TYGER

> Physicists at CERN, the Swiss particle physics laboratory, have created anti-atoms made of matter's opposite, anti-matter.

Anti-tyger Anti-tyger, burning bright,
In the anti-forests of the anti-night;
What immortal anti-hand or anti-eye
Could frame thy fearful anti-symmetry?

In what distant anti-deeps or anti-skies,
Burnt the anti-fire of thine anti-eyes?
On what anti-wings dare anti-he aspire?
What the anti-hand, dare seize the anti-fire?

And what anti-shoulder, & what anti-art,
Could twist the anti-sinews of thy anti-heart?
And when thy anti-heart began to beat,
What dread anti-hand? & what dread anti-feet?

What the anti-hammer? what the anti-chain,
In what anti-furnace was thy anti-brain?
What the anti-anvil? What dread anti-grasp,
Dare its deadly anti-terrors clasp?

When the anti-stars threw down their anti-spears
And water'd anti-heaven with their anti-tears:
Did anti-he smile his anti-work to see?
Did anti-he who made the anti-Lamb make anti-thee?

Anti-tyger Anti-tyger burning bright,
In the anti-forests of the anti-night:
What immortal anti-hand or anti-eye,
Dare frame thy fearful anti-symmetry?

THE GREATEST NAMES IN POETRY

Russell Banks

                Coleman Barks

                                Ellen Bass

Marvin Bell

                Wendell Berry

                                Elizabeth Bishop

David Bottoms

                Robert Bridges

                                Gwendolyn Brooks

Basil Bunting

                Robert Burns

                                Kelly Cherry

Wendy Cope

                Hart Crane

                                Stephen Crane

Rita Dove

                Edward Field

                                Carol Frost

Robert Frost

                Oliver Goldsmith

                                Robert Graves

Thomas Gray

        Barbara Guest

                Edgar Guest

Donald Hall

        Thomas Hood

                Donald Justice

Alicia Keys

        Etheridge Knight

                Thomas Lux

David Mason

        Edgar Lee Masters

                Howard Moss

Thylias Moss

        Octavio Paz

                Molly Peacock

Thomas Love Peacock

        Alexander Pope

                Ezra Pound

John Crowe Ransom

        David Ray

                Henry Reed

Ishmael Reed

        Adrienne Rich

                Robert Service

Anne Sexton

        Tom Sleigh

                Christopher Smart

Cathy Song

        Gerald Stern

                Ruth Stone

Mark Strand

        Jonathan Swift

                Madeline Tiger

Jean Valentine

        Robert Penn Warren

                Yvor Winters

THE HORSES

                Eight million died in World War I.

They would have needed 8,000,000 men
for one man to apologize to one horse.

When the men did not do so to one another,
where would they have found men to apologize to the horses?

It would have taken 8,000,000 Picassos
to do justice to the death agony of 8,000,000 horses.

Of the 8,000,000 horses, how many had names?
The Germans in particular targeted the horses.

When a British soldier's was killed or died,
he was required to cut off a hoof from his horse

to prove to his commanding officer that they
had not simply been separated, he and his horse.

Too tired to lift their heads high enough to breathe,
they drowned in the deep mud, thousands of the horses.

Because they were used to draw the artillery,
the most losses were suffered by the Clydesdale horses.

For some countries, the largest commodity
shipped to the front was fodder for the horses.

Because saw dust was mixed with their food,
they starved to death, thousands of the horses.

Gasmasks were issued for the horses,
but they destroyed them, mistaking them for feed bags.

The better-bred horses suffered from shell shock
more than the less well-bred horses.

These learned to lie down at the sound of the guns.
They were sold to the French butchers, the surviving horses.

THE LOVER OF STONE

The lover of stone must be old,
for there is no such thing as a young stone.

The lover of stone must be strong,
for he must able to climb up the mountain

and the summit of the mountain
to find the beginning of stone.

And he must be able to climb down
the mountain again to the valley

and to the bottom of the valley
to find the ending of stone.

The lover of stone must be a genius at unrequited love.
He must be an connoisseur of the cold.

The lover of stone must be a saint,
for stone will no more return his love

than does God return that of the saint.
The lover of stone must be jealous.

He must be jealous of the water that loves stone to smooth.
And he must be jealous of the wind that loves stone to death.

THE POEM OF THE FUTURE

The poem of the future will be smaller.
It will fit in the palm of your hand,
on your wrist, in your ear.

The poem of the future will not need
bulky batteries or cumbersome wires.
It will be powered by moonlight and weed.

The poem of the future will be automatic.
It will go for months without routine maintenance.
It will be faster, smoother, with a digital tick.

The poem of the future will be lighter.
It will be made of plastics and exotic metals.
It will be available in hundreds of shapes and colors.

The poem of the future will make our lives true.
It will perform in a second what it takes
the poem of the present a day to do.

The poem of the future will talk to us.
It will say things like "Buy IBM," and " Be my friend,"
and "Pulvis et umbra sumus."

TWO PORTRAITS BY MATHEW BRADY

1.
Here is Walt with his hat on his head,
his crumpled hat without a shape,
his rumpled, comfortable, free-verse hat on his head.
He looks as though he has just come in
from the rain and has suddenly sat down without being asked.
He looks like a grandfather, Walt does.
Better than that, Walt looks like a grandmother,
even with the beard, a grandmother, kindly and wise.
Walt has his hands in his pockets.
He looks as though he has just come in from the rain
and has sat down in front of the camera
without being asked and without taking his hat off
and without taking his hands from his pockets.
Walt fills the chair completely.
Walt sits in the chair as though sauntering down the street.
You cannot see Walt's hands and you cannot see
the chair because he fills it completely.
What a perfectly natural pose
for kindly, wise, grandmotherly, comfortable Walt.
Walt looks at you.
Walt looks right at you and no one else.
That's where Walt's eyes are: right in your eyes.

2.
It is hard to look at Hawthorne without getting hurt.
Everything about Hawthorne is hard.
Everything about Hawthorne hurts.
His hat is a stiff, black, formal, silk top-hat.
It looks like an iron cylinder in an iron ring.
It sits on a book, not on his head.
The book must be the bible, Hawthorne's bible or Brady's bible.
The bible sits on a table.
The book, the hat, the table are the props it hurts to look at.
Hawthorne's hands are clearly visible.
His right hand is clenched in a fist on the table.
It looks as though he has been pounding on the table.

His left hand grasps the arm of the chair.
Hawthorne looks as though he's been sitting in the chair all his life.
The chair is visible because Hawthorne does not fill it completely.
Hawthorne's hands are hard to look at.
Hawthorne looks like a preacher.
He looks stiff and uneasy and uncomfortable.
He looks as though there is something about the camera he is afraid of.
Hawthorne looks as though he were propped up with iron rings.
Hawthorne looks like his hat.
He is hard to look at.
He looks like a preacher who doesn't know
what to do with his hands because there's no lectern to hold.
Hawthorne looks over your shoulder.
His eyes are on the shadow over your shoulder.

WHEN THE BUDDHA WAS 80 YEARS OLD

When the Buddha was 80 years old
and about to die, he said
to his followers,
Make of yourself a light.
It is not recorded
that one leaned over
and whispered in his ear,
Enlightened One, tell us,
is it not also good
to make of yourself
the reflection of a light?
The Buddha's answer
was likewise not passed down.
It was: *Yes, that is also good.*

WORSE

> One could do worse than be a swinger of birches.

For example, one could be a slinger of burgers at McDonald's.
Or one could be a bringer of frivolous lawsuits.
Or one could be a flinger of gossipy dirt for *The New York Post*.

Or one could be a singer of inane songs on MTV for pre-teens.
Or one could be a clinger of apron strings.
Or one could be a dead-ringer for one of the FBI's *Ten Most Wanted*.

Or one could be a hunch-backed ringer of French church bells.
Or one could be a second-stringer on a last place minor league baseball team.
Or one could be a stringer for a newspaper in the sticks.

Or one could be a finger man for the mafia.
Or one could be a dinger of car fenders the parking lot of Walmart.
Or one could be a left-winger for a last place minor league hockey team.

Or one could be a right-winger of any country's politics.
Or one could be a jingler of idiotic jingles on the radio for pre-teens.
Or one could be a malingerer.

A YOUNG POET AND AN OLD POET

A young poet brought some poems he had written to an old poet he respected. The poems were full of airy sentiments, vagueness and philosophical generalities. The old poet read the poems with patience. Every so often he made a barely audible humming sound. Then he gave the poems back to the young poet and said, *A poem must have a body as well as a soul.* The young poet went home to his room where he tore up the poems. He put the pieces in a bowl. Then he wrote new poems, which, on the next day, he brought to the old poet he respected. These new poems were full of very specific details, the names of things both natural and man-made, and much matter-of-factness. The old poet read the poems with patience. Every so often he made a barely audible humming sound. Then he gave the poems back to the young poet and said, *A poem must have a soul as well as a body.* The young poet went home to his room where he tore up the poems. He put the pieces in the bowl that held the pieces of the old poems he had torn up. He mixed the pieces together and spilled them out onto the table. He glued the pieces together and the next day brought them to the old poet he respected. The old poet did not have to read the poems because he could see what the young poet had done. He saw that pieces did not fit. He said, *A poem must have a body and a soul with no space or seam between them.* The young poet was despondent. He went home and threw the poems in the river. A year later, while walking by the shore of the ocean, the young poet saw something in the water. He bent over and picked it up. It was a shell with paper inside. On the paper was written a poem. The young poet brought it to the old poet he respected. The old poet read the poem and right away said, *This is a poem. Hang it out on a pine branch to dry.*

TWENTY-TWO ATTEMPTS AT THE WILLIAM MATTHEWS CHALLENGE TO RUIN, WITH THE LEAST POSSIBLE CHANGE, A FAMOUS LINE OF POETRY

1.
Whose woods these are I think I know.
Whose irons these are I think I know.

2.
I heard a Fly Buzz – when I died –
I heard a Fly Buzz – when it died –

3.
The proper study of mankind is Man.
The proper study of mankind is jazz, man.

4.
Let us go then, you and I
Let us go then, me and you

5.
Little Lamb, who made thee?
Little Goat, who made thee?

6.
In Xanadu did Kubla Khan
In Timbuktu did Kubla Khan

7.
When I was one and twenty
When I was twenty-one

8.
I caught a tremendous fish

I caught a whopper

9.
"O where ha' you been, Lord Randall, my son?"

"O where ha' you been, Lord Sheldon, my son?"

10.
When I heard the learn'd astronomer

When I heard the learn'd astrologer

11.
About suffering they were never wrong

About surfing they were never wrong

12.
A poem should be palpable and mute

A poem should be palpable and cute

13.
Drink to me only with thine eyes

Blink to me only with thine eyes

14.
I felt a Funeral, in my Brain

I felt a Funeral, in my Spleen

15.
There were three ravens sat on a tree

There were three mavens sat on a tree

16.
When I see birches bend to left and right
When I see bitches bend to left and right

17.
Two roads diverged in a yellow wood
Two toads diverged in a yellow wood

18.
O Rose, thou art sick!
O Nose, thou art sick!

19.
Something there is that doesn't love a wall
Something there is that doesn't love a mall

20.
Gather ye rose-buds while ye may
Gather ye nose-bugs while ye may

21.
Do not go gentle into that good night.
Do not go, gentile, into that good night.

22.
How do I love thee? Let me count the ways.
How do I love thee? Let me count the lays.

IF EDGAR ALLAN POE HAD WRITTEN *"TREES"*

Once upon a midnight dreary, while I pondered, weak and weary,
While I thought that I should never see
A poem lovely, quaint and curious as a tree,
While I nodded, nearly napping, suddenly there came a tapping,
As of someone gently rapping, rapping at my chamber door.
                                        Quoth the Robin, "Nevermore!"

And the Robin, never flitting, still is sitting, still is sitting,
Upon the pallid bust and bosom just above my chamber door.
And his eyes have all the seeming intimately of rain is dreaming.
"Wretch," I cried. "Poems are made by fools like me.
Take thy beak from out my heart, and take thy nest from off my door!"
                                          Quoth the Robin, "Nevermore!"

IF WALLACE STEVENS HAD WRITTEN "*TREES*"

I   Among twenty snowy bosoms,
       The only moving thing
       Was the eye of the robin.

II   I was of three nests
       Like a tree
       In which there are three robins.

III   The robin whirled in the Summer rain.
       It was a small part of the prayer.

IV   A poet and a fool
       Are one.
       A poet and a fool and a robin
       Are one.

V   I do not know which to prefer,
       The lovely inflections
       Or the lovely innuendoes,
       The robin whistling
       Or just after.

VI   Icicles filled the long window
       With leafy arms.
       The shadow of the robin
       Crossed it, to and fro.
       The mouth
       Traced in the shadow
       Was in a hungry mood.

VII   O thin fools of the Bronx,
       Why do you imagine golden birds?
       Do you not see how the robin
       Walks around the feet
       Of the women about you?

VIII   I know ignoble accents
And inescapable meter;
But I know, too,
That the robin is involved
In what I know.

IX   When the robin flew out of sight,
It marked the edge
Of one of many breasts.

X   At the sight of robins
Flying in a green light,
Even the bawds of doggerel
Would cry out intimately.

XI   He rode over Fordham Road
In a glass nest.
Once, a fear pierced him.
In that he mistook
The shadow of his equipage
For robins.

XII   The river is moving.
The robins must be flying.

XIII   It was evening all afternoon.
It was raining
And it was going to rain.
God sat
In the maple-limbs.

IF ROBERT FROST HAD WRITTEN "*TREES*"

When I think that I shall never see
a birch tree bend to left and right,
I like to think some boy's been swinging it,
some boy whose hungry mouth is pressed
against the earth's sweet flowing breast
like the summer girls have, who on hands and knees,
throw their hair with nests of robins before them,
or like the girls of winter upon whose bosoms snow has lain,
and ice, too. That would be heaven. No foolin'.
Oh God, one could do worse than be
a swinger of a birch tree.

IF EMILY DICKINSON HAD WRITTEN "*TREES*"

I think that I shall
Never see a Poem—
As lovely as a Moor—
In a—Tree.

Yet I am Hungry—
To know how the Heather looks—
And just how leafy Arms—
Can pray—All day!
I never spoke—with God—
Nor visited a Robin's nest—Tee Hee!
Yet certain am—am I no fool—
That only He—
God, I mean—not Robin—
Can make a—Tree.

IF WALT WHITMAN HAD WRITTEN "*TREES*"

I sing the tree electric!
O tree! I believe the likes of you shall stand
Or fall with my poems, and that you are my poems.

Bark, trunk, roots, thick branches, more slender branches,
Branching branches and twigs, heartwood, sap, leaves, veins of leaves,
Rain on the canopy of leaves and on the veins of leaves,
Rain on the trunk, on the thick and slender branches,
And on the branching branches and twigs,
On the twigging branches, and on the twigs twigging outward, ever outward!
Then down into the roots encompassed by the rich earth,
Then the sap itself, blood of the tree, enriched by the rain,
Finally exhaled back into the air from whence it was born, exhausted,
And thence into myself, my own lungs and lung sacs,
My own capillaries, arteries, and veins, my own heartwood,
Bone, muscle, tendon, gristle, skin, follicles of hairs,
Coursing throughout, enriching all.

O I say not only, not only can a tree make such electricity!
O I say these are not the parts and poems of the tree only,
But of the soul,
O I say now these are the soul!

IF WILLIAM BLAKE HAD WRITTEN "*TREES*"

Robyn Robyn burning bright
In the forests of the treey night,
What immortal hand or eye
Could frame thy lovely symmetry?

What hungry mouth is press't
Against what flowing breast?
What leafy arms can pray?
What looks at God all day?

Upon whose bosom has lain snow?
With rain so intimately be?
And what damn'd fool wants to know
If only He who made the Lamb can make a tree?

IF T.S ELIOT HAD WRITTEN "*TREES*"

April is the cruelest month, breeding
Peach trees—Do I dare to eat one?—out
Of the dead land, mixing
Hungry mouth and flowing breast, stirring
A nest of robins with spring rain.
Winter kept us warm, covering
Earth's bosom in forgetful snow, feeding
A little fool like Pru with dried poems.

A PHOTOGRAPH OF CHARLIE CHAPLIN AND ALBERT EINSTEIN

Although it looks as if they're only sharing a dirty joke,
still one wonders what they're talking about,

these two world-champion tramps,
physicist and funnyman,

shoulder to shoulder, smiling for the camera,
foundling brothers reunited

after living all their lives apart,
posing like ancient tribal enemies caught

in the act of compromise at this
their secret summit of the sublime and the ridiculous,

discovered now as though the gods,
jealous of such shocking amity,

had blackmail on their minds.
But they know better, standing together

like a bad rhyme,
their twinkling eyes admitting zero

but universal laughter,
ridiculous and sublime.

OVER THERE

Although we know they may
not be better necessarily,
over there we know at least
things are different, and we

sense we would be different
ourselves all these years
had we been born, brought
up, nurtured over there,

been given opportunities
to play the barefoot games,
had we had the friends
with the perfect trochee names

who lived on streets with
no sharp corners but with trees
that grew, merged over roads,
melded light like arches,

in houses shadowed with
pianos and portraits in oil,
who went to the alabaster
school on the low, smooth hill

with a library on whose
shelves are only first editions
bound in leather and halls
echoing a bronze tradition

like a language stranger
than ours, older and stronger,
the language of flawless children
into which ours fades forever.

ANGINA

It is a hand on the heart,
a greeting.
It is mortality grinning,
dumbly, with its big,

hearty hand on the heart,
mortality in person,
squeezing the heart
with its big, hot hand.

And then it becomes
remembering,
the heart remembering
painful experiences

from its infancy,
its childhood and its youth,
separations in the dark,
nightmares of falling

and chases through forests,
unrequited love for heroines
of books and movie stars,
an ache in the shape

of a hand holding such
a heavy heart heart-level
and too long to bear.
It is Latin for *torture*.

PERCY SHELLEY TO A SKYLARK

(From a List of Related Searches)

To a skylark,
Percy Shelley is just anybody lying

on his back on the grass,
his head in some woman's lap,

tapping a pencil against her thigh,
tah ta dah ta tah dah dah ta tah dah dah.

Percy Shelley to a skylark?
Nothing special.

SCHOPENHAUER AT THE ENGLISCHER HOF

A Monologue

I have been called a pessimist. I am.
What man who calls himself a thoughtful man,
a feeling man, can be ought else? The wine?
The wine is good, but I prefer the beer.
I took no wife because I wanted none.
I live alone because I wish to live
alone. The passions must be overcome.
I recommend the veal. It's excellent.
The monarchs made a mockery of hope.
My father was a businessman. He killed
himself when I was seventeen. I left
my mother's house soon afterward because
she chose a life I could not tolerate
to look upon. She was a novelist,
you know, received the intellectuals
of Weimar in her parlor. And her bed.
She let old Goethe bring his Christiane
with him, but when he told her I, her son,
would be a very famous man, she pushed
me down the stairs. Her name is only known
through me, the bitch. Who reads her novels now?
I come to dine here almost every day.
Before I start I place a coin – this one –
beside the plate, and when I'm done, I put
the coin back in my pocket once again.
It is a wager that I've made myself
to drop it in the poor box of the church
the day the English officers who dine
at this establishment should talk of else
than horses, women, or dogs. Here, I have
one. His name is *Atma*. It means World- Soul.
Why was my masterpiece unrecognized?
Because just those who could have given it
publicity – the university
philosophers – I have attacked in it.

Ah, yes, good man, the veal for both of us.
The rule, *I sing the song of him whose bread
I eat,* has always held. It now, too, holds.
I make no living from philosophy.
I have inherited an interest in
my father's firm, and that has been enough.
The life of every individual,
when we survey it as a whole and stress
its most important parts, is tragedy.
But in the details, always comedy.
The world is bankrupt in the end, and life's
a business which does not recoup expense.
All happiness requires ignorance
or youth, for youth and ignorance are one.
The fear of death is the beginning of
philosophy, religion's final cause.
Diogenes refused to breathe – and died.
A brilliant victory! Alas, how vain.
The more things change, the more they stay the same.
This is the essence of philosophy.
The true philosophy of history
lies in perceiving this eternal truth.
In general, the wise have always said
the same. The fools have acted all alike
as well and done the opposite. And thus
reality is suffering and pain.
And thus the genius suffers most of all.
You hear? You hear the English gentlemen?
The coin is in my pocket once again.

ONE OF THE TRAPPED CHILEAN MINERS WAS A POET

Do not send down for me.
Instead send down the food and the drink.
Send down the clean bed-pans.
Send down the pencils and the paper.
Send down the wooden flute.
My eyes are used to the dark.
I'm staying here.

Do not send down for me.
Instead send down the clean bed-pans.
Send down the food and the drink.
Send down the pencils and the paper.
Send down the wooden flute.
My ears are used to my heartbeat.
I'm staying here.

Do not send down for me.
Instead send down the pencils and the paper.
Send down the food and the drink.
Send down the clean bed-pans.
Send down the wooden flute.
My mouth is used to my voice.
I'm staying here.

Do not send down for me.
Instead send down the wooden flute.
Send down the food and the drink.
Send down the clean bed-pans.
Send down the pencils and the paper.
My soul is used to my body.
I'm staying here.

Do not send down for me.
I'm staying here.
The earth is used to me.

ZEPPO

They say he was the funniest
of the four. We'll never know.

In an early film (perhaps to test
just how far they would let him go),

he ad-libs a joke. Groucho,
visibly annoyed, throws a snap

at him as he walks off. At best
he was handsome and sang. A trap.

Invariably they would merely send
him away. But he got the girl in the end.

www.ingramcontent.com/pod-product-compliance
Lightning Source LLC
Chambersburg PA
CBHW071753080526
44588CB00013B/2227